Sagittarius
Astrology Coloring Book

Color Your Zodiac Sign

DYLANNA PRESS

Copyright © 2020 by Dylanna Press
All rights reserved.

The 12 Signs

Sign Symbols

ARIES

TAURUS

GEMINI

CANCER

LEO

VIRGO

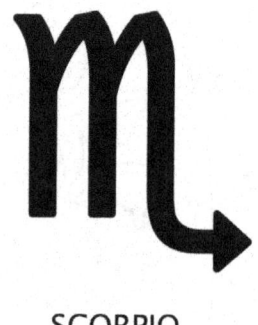

LIBRA

SCORPIO

SAGITTARIUS

CAPRICORN

AQUARIUS

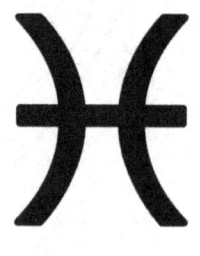

PISCES

Sagittarius

November 22 - December 21

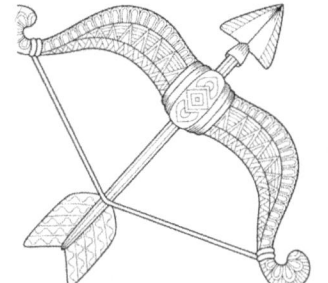

SAGITTARIUS ARE the open-minded travelers of the zodiac. With a love for freedom, the outdoors, and philosophy they long to search the world for the meaning of life. They are generally optimistic, energetic, and humorous. Jupiter is the largest planet and rules over this sign providing them with a feeling of abundance. Freedom is their greatest desire; however, they are often impatient and undiplomatic because of this. They often live dynamic and exciting lives as photographers, travel writers, artists, and things of a similar nature.

Symbol: Archer

Planet: Jupiter

Element: Fire

Color: Blue

Traits: Generous, Humorous, Idealistic, Optimistic, Honest, Impatient, Rebellious

Constellation:

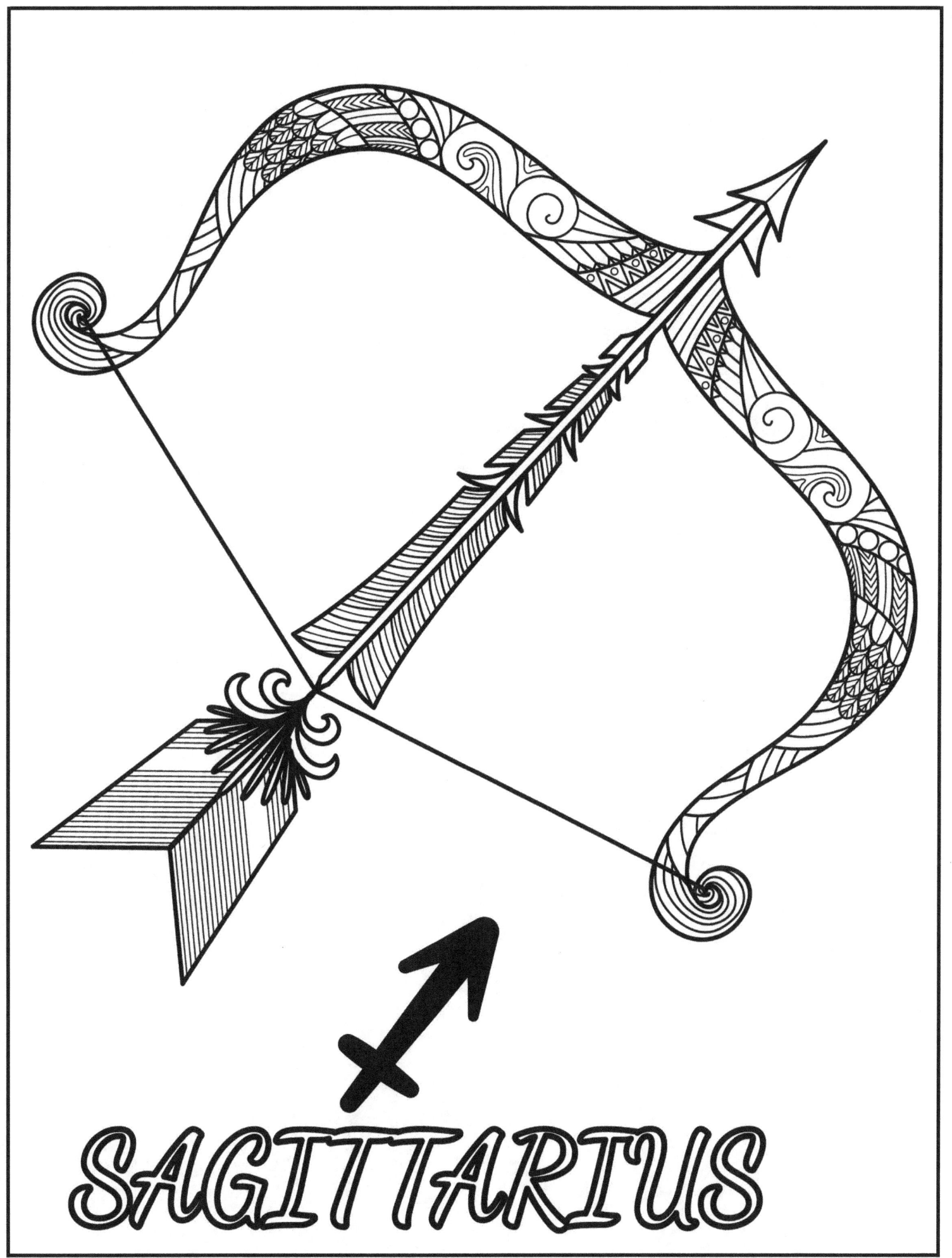

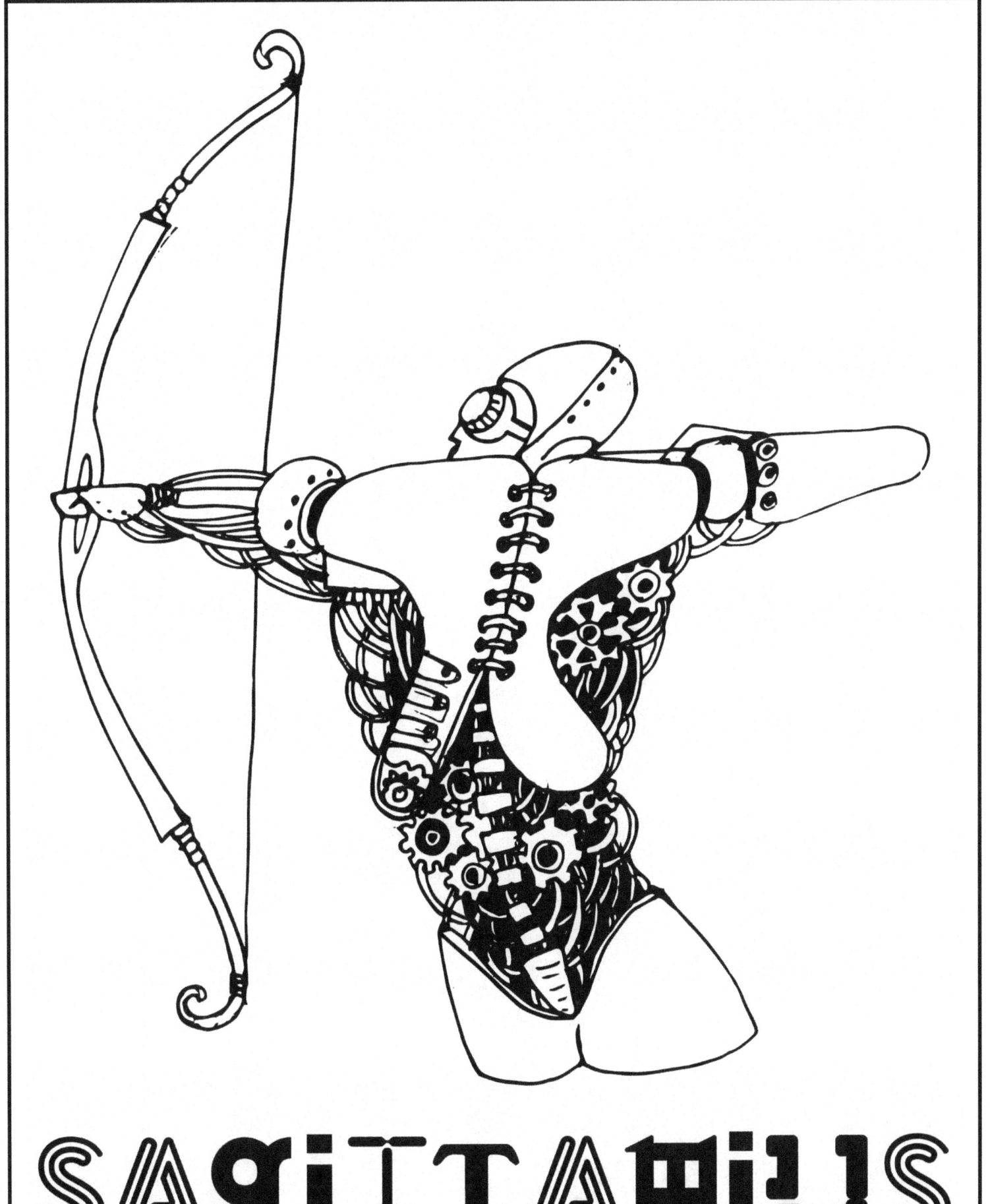